HOW TO GET
FINANCIALLY INDEPENDENT AT AN EARLY AGE

JASDEEP CHAWLA

BLUEROSE PUBLISHERS
India | U.K.

Copyright © Jasdeep Chawla 2024

All rights reserved by author. No part of this publication may be reproduced, stored in a retrieval system or transmitted in any form or by any means, electronic, mechanical, photocopying, recording or otherwise, without the prior permission of the author. Although every precaution has been taken to verify the accuracy of the information contained herein, the publisher assumes no responsibility for any errors or omissions. No liability is assumed for damages that may result from the use of information contained within.

BlueRose Publishers takes no responsibility for any damages, losses, or liabilities that may arise from the use or misuse of the information, products, or services provided in this publication.

For permissions requests or inquiries regarding this publication, please contact:

BLUEROSE PUBLISHERS
www.BlueRoseONE.com
info@bluerosepublishers.com
+91 8882 898 898
+4407342408967

ISBN: 978-93-6261-485-8

Cover design: Rishav Rai
Typesetting: Rohit

First Edition: May 2024

Introduction

Finance is an important aspect of our lives, yet many people find it difficult to understand. This book is designed to provide a comprehensive overview of finance for everyone. Whether you are new to investing or just want to improve your financial literacy, this book will cover the basics of finance and help you make informed decisions about your money.

Contents

1. Understanding the Basics of Finance 1
2. Budgeting and Saving 6
3. Banking and Credit 11
4. Investing 15
5. Retirement Planning 19
6. Real Estate Investing Understanding Real Estate Investing 26
7. Taxes 30
8. Financial Planning 35

Conclusion 39

Chapter 1

Understanding the Basics of Finance

Finance is a field that deals with the study of money management, including the allocation, investment, and management of financial resources. It involves the creation and analysis of financial statements, the development of investment strategies, and the management of financial risk.

Finance is important for individuals, businesses, and governments to make informed decisions about how to use and manage their financial resources effectively. It covers a wide range of topics such as budgeting, saving, banking, credit, investing, retirement planning, real estate investing, taxes, and financial planning.

In essence, finance is the art of effectively managing finances and making informed decisions rooted in thorough analysis, risk evaluation, and goal establishment. It equips individuals and entities alike with the necessary tools and insights to navigate towards their financial aspirations, fostering a sturdy foundation for a prosperous future.

* Importance of finance

Finance plays a crucial role in our daily lives and has significant importance in various areas, such as personal finance, business finance, and government finance. Some of the key aspects of finance are:

1. Management of money: Finance provides individuals, businesses, and governments with the tools and knowledge

necessary to manage their money efficiently, including budgeting, investing, and financial planning.

2. Investment: Finance helps individuals and organisations make informed investment decisions based on analysis and risk assessment, which can lead to higher returns and long-term financial stability.

3. Economic growth: Finance contributes to economic growth by providing businesses with the necessary capital to grow and expand, creating jobs, and generating income.

4. Financial stability: Finance is essential for maintaining financial stability at both the individual and institutional levels, protecting against financial risks

5. International trade and commerce: Finance facilitates international trade and commerce by providing businesses with the necessary financial instruments and services to conduct transactions across borders

Finance is crucial for achieving financial stability, promoting economic growth, and making informed financial decisions at both the personal and institutional levels.

In the bustling suburbs of Oakville, lived a 16-year-old teenager named Emily Carson. Unlike most teens her age, Emily wasn't content with a weekly allowance. She harbored a dream of amassing wealth through smart investments, a dream that seemed audacious but not impossible. Emily embarked on her journey with nothing but a simple lemonade stand. Every weekend was dedicated to squeezing lemons, blending sugar, and perfecting her lemonade concoction. Through sheer determination and frugality, she managed to turn her humble stand into a beloved local attraction, showcasing the power of hard work and perseverance. Gradually, as her lemonade profits grew, Emily's curiosity turned towards the stock market. She began devouring books on finance and trading, using her earnings to buy her first few shares of stock.

The stock market became her classroom, and every gain or loss was a lesson.

After years of diligent saving and learning, Emily had amassed a significant sum. At the age of 18, she made her first significant investment, buying shares in a promising tech startup. The investment paid off handsomely, catapulting her net worth into a new league.

The earlier you start , the earlier you get rich. There is no such thing as getting rich quickly, but when you learn about compounding at an early age, it feels like you have learned magic.

Take the example of Sarah and John

In the world of finance, there's a timeless story that beautifully illustrates the concept of compounding and the profound impact of investing early. Let me share it with you.

Meet Sarah and John, childhood friends who embarked on their financial journeys at the age of 20.

Sarah was a diligent saver. She decided to invest $2,000 every year in a well-diversified portfolio of stocks and continued to do so until she turned 30. After that, she stopped contributing but let her investments grow.

John, on the other hand, procrastinated for a decade. He didn't start investing until he was 30, and he also invested $2,000 per year into a similar portfolio of stocks. Unlike Sarah, John remained consistent, investing $2,000 each year until he reached the age of 60.

Now, let's fast forward to their 60th birthdays and see how their financial journeys unfolded.

Sarah's investments had 30 years to compound and grow. By the time she turned 60, her portfolio had grown significantly, reaching a total value of $283,355. Not bad for a decade of saving and three decades of compounding.

John, despite investing for three decades, found himself with a smaller portfolio. His investments had 30 years to grow, but they couldn't quite catch up to Sarah's due to the late start. John's portfolio was worth $215,866, about $67,489 less than Sarah's.

This story perfectly illustrates the power of compounding and the importance of starting early. Sarah, who started investing in her 20s and then stopped, ended up with more money than John, who invested for a longer duration but started a decade later. It serves as a compelling reminder that time is your greatest ally when it comes to building wealth through investing. Starting early can make all the difference in the world of finance.

* The time value of money

The time value of money (TVM) is a fundamental concept in finance that refers to the idea that a dollar today is worth more than a dollar received in the future. This is because of the opportunity cost of not having that dollar today and the potential to invest that dollar and earn interest or returns.

The concept of TVM is based on two key principles:

1. Future cash flows are worth less than present cash flows: Due to inflation and the potential to invest money today and earn interest, future cash flows are worth less than the same amount of money received today.

2. The value of money changes over time: The purchasing power of money changes over time due to inflation, currency exchange rates, and other factors.

To account for the time value of money, financial professionals employ various tools and techniques, such as discounted cash flow analysis, net present value (NPV), and internal rate of return (IRR) calculations.

These tools allow for the comparison of cash flows at different points in time and help in making informed financial decisions.

Understanding the time value of money is crucial for individuals and businesses alike when making decisions about borrowing, investing, and saving. By taking into account the time value of money, individuals and businesses can make informed financial decisions that are aligned with their long-term goals and objectives.

Chapter 2

Budgeting and Saving

* The importance of budgeting

Budgeting is the process of creating a plan for how to spend and allocate financial resources over a specific period, usually monthly, quarterly, or annually. Budgeting is a critical component of financial management and has several important benefits, including:

1. Control over spending: Budgeting helps individuals and businesses keep track of their expenses and provides a framework for managing spending. This helps prevent overspending, reduces debt, and allows for better financial management.

2. Goal setting: Budgeting allows individuals and businesses to set financial goals, such as saving for a down payment on a house or paying off debt. By setting specific goals, budgeting helps individuals and businesses prioritize their spending and allocate resources accordingly.

3. Decision-making: Budgeting provides a framework for making financial decisions, such as whether to invest in a new project or purchase a new asset. By providing a clear picture of financial resources, budgeting helps individuals and businesses make informed decisions.

4. Forecasting: Budgeting allows individuals and businesses to forecast future expenses and income, which is useful in long-term planning. This practice assists individuals and businesses in

anticipating unforeseen events, such as sudden rises in expenses or declines in income, by ensuring they have adequate financial reserves and contingency plans in place.

5. Financial accountability: Budgeting helps individuals and businesses be financially accountable by tracking expenses and ensuring that financial resources are used effectively and efficiently.

In summary, budgeting is a critical component of financial management that helps individuals and businesses control spending, set goals, make informed decisions, forecast future expenses, and be financially accountable. By creating and following a budget, individuals and businesses can achieve financial stability and work towards their long-term financial goals.

1. Setting financial goals can help you achieve greater financial security and freedom. Here are some easy steps to help you set financial goals:

2. Determine your financial priorities: Decide what is most important to you and what you want to achieve. For example, you may want to save for a down payment on a house, pay off debt, or build an emergency fund.

3. Set specific goals: Make sure your goals are specific, measurable, and achievable. For example, instead of saying, "I want to save money," set a goal to save $5,000 by the end of the year.

4. Create a plan: Once you have your goals, create a plan for achieving them. This may involve creating a budget, cutting expenses, increasing your income, or investing.

5. Track your progress: Regularly track your progress towards your goals to ensure you are on track. You can use tools like spreadsheets or budgeting apps to help you keep track of your spending and progress towards your goals.

6. Celebrate your successes: When you reach a milestone or achieve a goal, take time to celebrate your success. This can help motivate you to continue working towards your other financial goals

Sarah was meticulous in her approach. She tracked every expense, from her morning coffee to her monthly rent. She created a comprehensive budget that allocated a portion of her income to savings, bills, and discretionary spending. Sarah's budgeting discipline allowed her to live comfortably while still saving for her future goals.

John, initially skeptical about budgeting, decided to give it a try after seeing Sarah's progress. However, his approach was less detailed. He created a basic budget, focusing mainly on his fixed expenses and ignoring smaller discretionary spending.

As the months rolled by, both Sarah and John faced unexpected expenses. Sarah, with her well- documented budget, was prepared. She had an emergency fund in place, ready to cover unexpected car repairs and medical bills without derailing her financial plan.

John, on the other hand, struggled when unexpected expenses arose. He dipped into his savings, which he had neglected to designate as an emergency fund, causing stress and uncertainty.

Over time, Sarah's budgeting prowess allowed her to achieve her financial goals. She saved for a dream vacation, paid off her student loans, and even started investing for her retirement.

John, while realizing the importance of budgeting, decided to adopt Sarah's meticulous approach. He began tracking all expenses, building an emergency fund, and saving for specific goals. With time, his financial situation improved, and he, too, started achieving his aspirations.

Sarah and John highlight the transformative power of budgeting. Sarah's dedication and attention to detail led her to financial stability and success. John's initial resistance taught him that a well-structured budget can be a lifeline in times of uncertainty and a roadmap to achieving his dreams.

* Creating a budget

* Planning a budget is an essential aspect of financial management. It involves taking stock of your income, expenses, and debts to create a plan that enables you to achieve your financial goals. The first step in planning a budget is to identify your sources of income, including your salary, investment income, and any other sources of regular income. Next, you should make a list of all your expenses, including your rent or mortgage, utilities, groceries, transportation, and any other recurring expenses. It is also essential to account for any debts you may have, such as credit card debt or student loans. Once you have a clear understanding of your income and expenses, you can create a budget that allocates your income to your expenses, savings, and debt payments. A well-planned budget can help you achieve your financial goals, such as paying off debt, saving for retirement, or building an emergency fund.

Regularly monitoring and adjusting your budget can help you stay on track and ensure that you are making progress towards your financial goals.

* **Tips for saving money**
*

1. Set financial goals: Determine what you want to achieve financially, and set clear, specific, and achievable goals.

2. Track your spending: Track all your expenses to know where your money is going. This will help you identify areas where you can cut back on spending.

3. Create a budget: Use the information you gathered from tracking your expenses to create a realistic budget. Make sure to

include all your expenses, such as rent, utilities, groceries, transportation, and entertainment.

4. Automate your savings: Set up automatic transfers from your checking account to a savings account. This way, you won't have to worry about remembering to save money each month.

5. Reduce your debt: Pay off your debts as soon as possible. This will not only improve your credit score but also free up money that can be put towards savings.

6. Look for ways to save: Look for ways to save money on everyday expenses. For example, you could switch to a cheaper phone plan, buy generic products instead of branded products, or use coupons.

7. Avoid impulse purchases: Before making a purchase, ask yourself if you really need the item. If it is not essential, consider waiting a few days to see if you still want it.

8. Invest wisely: Consider investing your money in low-cost index funds or other investment vehicles that offer a reasonable rate of return.

9. Stay motivated: Stay motivated by reminding yourself of your financial goals and the progress you've made. Celebrate small milestones and keep working towards your long-term goals.

Chapter 3

Banking and Credit

* **Understanding different types of bank accounts**

* Here are some of the most common types of bank accounts and what they are typically used for:

1. Checking Accounts: A checking account is a bank account that allows you to deposit and withdraw money easily. It is used for day-to-day transactions, such as paying bills, writing checks, and using a debit card for purchases. Checking accounts usually offer limited or no interest on the balance.

2. Savings Accounts: A savings account is a bank account that allows you to earn interest on the money you deposit. It is usually ideal for long-term savings goals, such as building an emergency fund or saving for a down payment on a house. Savings accounts often have limits on the number of withdrawals or transfers per month.

3. Money Market Accounts: A money market account is a type of savings account that offers a higher interest rate in exchange for a higher minimum balance. Money market accounts often have limited check-writing capabilities, but they typically offer higher interest rates than traditional savings accounts.

* Choosing the right bank

* Choosing the right bank is important for several reasons. Firstly, the bank you choose can have an impact on your financial

stability and security. A reputable and trustworthy bank will provide you with a safe place to store your money and protect it from fraud or theft. On the other hand, a less reliable bank may not have the necessary security measures in place to keep your funds safe.

* Secondly, the bank you choose can affect your overall financial health. Different banks offer different interest rates on savings accounts and loans, and choosing the right bank can help you save money in the long run. A bank with high-interest rates on savings accounts, for example, can help you grow your wealth over time.

* Finally, the services and products offered by different banks can vary widely. Some banks offer specialized services such as investment advice or business loans, while others may focus more on consumer banking. By choosing the right bank, you can ensure that you have access to the products and services that are most important to you.

* Overall, choosing the right bank is an important decision that can have a significant impact on your financial well-being.

* Managing your credit score

* Managing your credit score is important for several reasons. Your credit score is a numerical representation of your creditworthiness and is used by lenders, landlords, and even potential employers to evaluate your financial responsibility. A high credit score can open doors to better interest rates on loans and credit cards, while a low credit score can make it difficult to obtain credit or get approved for a rental property.

* Maintaining a good credit score requires careful management of your credit accounts. This includes paying your bills on time, keeping your credit card balances low, and avoiding opening too many new credit accounts at once. By doing so, you can demonstrate to lenders that you are responsible with credit and can be trusted to repay loans on time.

* Additionally, monitoring your credit score regularly can help you detect and address any errors or fraudulent activity on your credit report. This can help you avoid negative impacts on your credit score and protect yourself from identity theft.

* In summary, managing your credit score is essential for maintaining financial health and achieving your financial goals. It can help you secure favorable interest rates, access credit and rental opportunities, and protect yourself from fraud and errors on your credit report.

* Understanding credit cards

A credit card is a payment card that allows you to borrow money from a financial institution to make purchases. When you use a credit card, you are essentially taking out a loan that must be repaid with interest.

Credit cards typically have a credit limit, which is the maximum amount you can borrow at any given time. Your credit limit is determined by your creditworthiness, income, and other factors. You can use your credit card to make purchases up to your credit limit, and you can repay the balance in full or make minimum payments over time.

Credit cards often come with rewards or cash back programs that allow you to earn points or cash back on purchases. These rewards can be redeemed for travel, merchandise, or statement credits.

Using a credit card responsibly is important to maintain good credit and avoid debt. It is recommended to pay your credit card balance in full each month to avoid interest charges and late fees. It is also important to avoid overspending and to stay within your budget.

If you are unable to make payments on your credit card, your account may become delinquent, and your credit score may be negatively impacted. In extreme cases, credit card debt can lead to bankruptcy.

In summary, credit cards can be a convenient and useful tool for making purchases and earning rewards, but it is important to use them responsibly and avoid overspending.

Chapter 4

Investing

Types of investments (stocks, bonds, and mutual funds)

There are several types of investments, including stocks, bonds, and mutual funds.

Stocks represent ownership in a company and provide the potential for capital gains if the company's value increases. However, stocks can also be volatile, and their value can fluctuate based on a variety of factors.

Bonds are debt securities issued by companies or governments, and they provide a fixed income stream in the form of interest payments. Bonds are generally considered less risky than stocks, but they also offer lower returns.

Mutual funds are investment vehicles that pool money from multiple investors to buy a diversified portfolio of stocks, bonds, or other securities. This allows investors to spread their risk and benefit from professional management. However, mutual funds can also come with fees and expenses that can eat into returns.

Choosing the right type of investment depends on an individual's financial goals, risk tolerance, and time horizon. It is important to carefully consider these factors and consult with a financial professional before making any investment decisions.

* **Assessing risk tolerance**

Assessing your risk tolerance is an important step in developing an investment strategy that aligns with your financial goals and comfort level. Risk tolerance refers to the degree of uncertainty or potential loss an investor is willing to accept in pursuit of higher returns.

There are several factors that can impact your risk tolerance, including your age, income, financial goals, and personal preferences. Some individuals may be comfortable taking on higher levels of risk in pursuit of higher returns, while others may prioritize the preservation of capital and be more risk-averse.

To assess your risk tolerance, you can start by considering your investment goals, time horizon, and financial situation. You may also want to consider your emotional reaction to market fluctuations and potential losses.

There are several tools and questionnaires available online that can help you assess your risk tolerance, but it is important to keep in mind that these tools are only a starting point and should not be relied on as the sole basis for investment decisions.

Ultimately, determining your risk tolerance is a personal decision that should take into account your individual circumstances and financial goals. It is important to work with a financial professional to develop an investment strategy that aligns with your risk tolerance and helps you achieve your long- term financial goals.

* **Diversification**

Diversification is a key principle of investment that involves spreading your investments across different asset classes, industries, and geographic regions. The goal of diversification is to reduce risk and protect your portfolio from potential losses by avoiding over-concentration in any one area.

When you diversify your investments, you spread your risk across a variety of assets that behave differently under different market conditions. For example, if you invest all of your money in a single stock, your portfolio is at risk if that company performs poorly. However, if you diversify across multiple stocks, bonds, and other securities, you can reduce the impact of any single investment on your overall portfolio.

Diversification can be achieved through various investment vehicles, such as mutual funds, exchange- traded funds (ETFs), and index funds. These funds offer a diversified portfolio of stocks or bonds, allowing investors to benefit from professional management and broad market exposure.

It is important to note that diversification does not guarantee profits or protect against losses. However, it can help manage risk and potentially increase long-term returns. By diversifying your investments, you can reduce the impact of market volatility and position your portfolio for long-term growth.

In summary, diversification is an important principle of investment that can help reduce risk and protect your portfolio from potential losses. By spreading your investments across different asset classes and industries, you can potentially increase returns and achieve long-term financial goals.

* **Strategies for Investing**

Several strategies for investing can help investors achieve their financial goals. Here are a few popular investment strategies:

1. Buy and hold: This strategy involves buying investments and holding them for the long term, usually several years or more. The goal is to ride out short-term market fluctuations and benefit from long-term growth.

2. Dollar-cost averaging: This strategy involves investing a fixed amount of money at regular intervals, regardless of market conditions. This can help smooth out the impact of market volatility and potentially generate better returns over time.

3. Value investing: This strategy involves identifying undervalued stocks or assets that are trading below their intrinsic value. The goal is to buy these assets at a discount and hold them until their value increases.

4. Growth investing: This strategy involves investing in companies that are expected to grow at a faster rate than the market average. The goal is to benefit from the potential for higher returns, although this strategy can also be riskier.

5. Index investing: This strategy involves investing in a portfolio of stocks or other assets that track a particular index, such as the S&P 500. The goal is to achieve broad market exposure and potentially benefit from long-term market growth.

Regardless of the strategy you choose, it is important to have a clear investment plan that aligns with your financial goals and risk tolerance. It is also important to diversify your investments and regularly review your portfolio to ensure it remains aligned with your goals and risk tolerance. Working with a financial professional can help you develop an investment strategy that is tailored to your individual circumstances and helps you achieve your long-term financial goals.

Chapter 5

Retirement Planning

* Understanding retirement plans (401k, IRA, etc.). Retirement plans are financial vehicles designed to help individuals save and invest for their retirement years. They offer tax advantages and various investment options to help grow your savings over time. Two common types of retirement plans in the United States are the 401(k) and the Individual Retirement Account (IRA). Here's an overview of each:

1. 401(k) Plan:

* A 401(k) is an employer-sponsored retirement plan offered by many companies.

* Contributions are made on a pre-tax basis, meaning they are deducted from your paycheck before taxes are applied.

* Employers often provide a matching contribution, where they contribute a percentage of your salary to your 401(k) based on your own contributions.

* Contributions and earnings grow tax-deferred until withdrawal. Taxes are only paid when you withdraw funds in retirement.

* There are limits to how much you can contribute each year, which are set by the Internal Revenue Service (IRS).

* Generally, you cannot withdraw funds from a 401(k) without penalty until you reach the age of 59½, although certain exceptions may apply.

2. Individual Retirement Account (IRA):

* An IRA is a personal retirement account that you can establish independently.

* There are two main types of IRAs: Traditional IRA and Roth IRA.

* Traditional IRA: Contributions are made with pre-tax dollars, and the earnings grow tax-deferred.

Withdrawals in retirement are subject to income tax.

* Roth IRA: Contributions are made with after-tax dollars, meaning you've already paid taxes on the money. The earnings grow tax-free, and qualified withdrawals in retirement are tax-free as well.

* Both Traditional and Roth IRAs have annual contribution limits set by the IRS.

* IRA accounts are self-directed, giving you more control over your investment choices compared to a 401(k).

* Other types of retirement plans include Simplified Employee Pension (SEP) IRAs, which are designed for self-employed individuals or small business owners, and Simple IRAs, which are retirement plans for small businesses with fewer than 100 employees.

* It is important to note that retirement plans can have specific rules and regulations, and individual circumstances may vary. It is advisable to consult with a financial advisor or tax professional to understand the specific details and options available to you based on your situation and goals.

* **Assessing retirement needs**

* Assessing your retirement needs involves estimating the amount of money you'll require to cover your expenses and maintain your desired lifestyle during retirement. While everyone's needs may vary, here are some key steps to help you assess your retirement needs:

1. Determine your desired retirement lifestyle: Start by envisioning how you want to spend your retirement years. Consider factors such as where you want to live, travel plans, hobbies, healthcare expenses, and any other significant lifestyle choices. This will help you estimate the level of income you'll need to support your desired lifestyle.

2. Estimate your retirement expenses: Calculate your projected expenses during retirement. Consider both essential expenses (housing, food, healthcare, and utilities) and discretionary expenses (travel, hobbies, and entertainment). Account for any expected changes, such as mortgage payments being paid off or healthcare costs increasing.

3. Consider inflation: Keep in mind that the cost of living typically increases over time due to inflation. When estimating your retirement expenses, factor in a reasonable inflation rate to ensure your income keeps pace with rising prices.

4. Assess potential sources of retirement income: Take stock of your potential sources of retirement income, such as Social Security benefits, pensions, and any other retirement accounts you've accumulated (e.g., 401(k), IRAs). Review the projected income you can expect from each source and factor it into your overall retirement plan.

5. Calculate the retirement savings needed: Once you have estimated your retirement expenses and considered your potential income sources, you can determine how much retirement savings you'll need. This can be done using retirement calculators or consulting with a financial advisor. They can help you factor in

variables such as investment returns, life expectancy, and any additional factors specific to your situation.

6. Regularly review and adjust your plan: It is important to regularly review your retirement plan and adjust it as needed. Life circumstances and financial goals may change over time, so staying proactive and making necessary adjustments can help you stay on track towards your retirement needs.

* Remember, retirement planning is a complex process, and individual circumstances may differ. Seeking guidance from a financial advisor can provide personalized insights and recommendations based on your specific situation, helping you create a more accurate assessment of your retirement needs.

* **Retirement savings strategies**

Certainly! Here's a summary of retirement savings strategies to help you plan for a secure retirement:

1. Start saving early: The power of compounding allows your savings to grow over time. The earlier you start, the more time your money has to grow. Consistent contributions over the long term can make a significant difference.

2. Maximize employer-sponsored plans: Take advantage of employer-sponsored retirement plans, such as a 401(k) or similar plans. Contribute at least enough to receive the maximum employer match, as it is essentially free money. Aim to increase your contributions over time as your financial situation allows.

3. Utilize individual retirement accounts (IRAs): Contribute to Traditional or Roth IRAs based on your eligibility. These accounts provide additional tax advantages and can supplement your employer- sponsored plan.

4. Create a diversified investment portfolio: Diversify your retirement investments across different asset classes (stocks, bonds, real estate, etc.) to manage risk and potentially increase returns.

Consider your risk tolerance, time horizon, and seek professional advice if needed.

5. Keep an eye on fees: Review the fees associated with your retirement accounts and investments. High fees can eat into your returns over time. Opt for low-cost investment options, such as index funds or exchange-traded funds (ETFs), when appropriate.

6. Regularly review and adjust your savings: Revisit your retirement savings strategy periodically. Adjust your contributions and investments as needed, considering factors like life changes, market conditions, and retirement goals.

7. Consider catch-up contributions: If you are over 50, take advantage of catch-up contributions allowed by retirement plans and IRAs. These allow you to contribute additional funds beyond the regular contribution limits.

8. Manage debt and expenses: Reduce and manage debt effectively to free up cash flow for retirement savings. Create a budget and look for opportunities to cut unnecessary expenses, directing those savings towards retirement.

9. Stay informed and seek professional advice: Stay updated on retirement planning best practices and changes to retirement laws. Consider consulting with a financial advisor who specializes in retirement planning to develop a personalized strategy.

Remember, everyone's financial situation and retirement goals are unique. Adjust these strategies to align with your specific needs, and regularly reassess your retirement savings plan as circumstances change.

* **Planning for unexpected expenses**

* Planning for unexpected expenses is an essential part of financial preparedness. Here are some strategies to help you navigate unexpected expenses like a pro:

1. Build an emergency fund: Establish an emergency fund specifically designated for unexpected expenses. Aim to save three to six months' worth of living expenses. This fund acts as a financial safety net, allowing you to cover unforeseen costs without derailing your long-term financial goals.

2. Review and adjust your budget: Regularly review your budget to identify areas where you can cut back or save more. Allocate a portion of your income towards building your emergency fund and addressing unexpected expenses.

3. Practice mindful spending: Cultivate a habit of mindful spending by distinguishing between needs and wants. Before making a purchase, evaluate whether it aligns with your priorities and if it is necessary. This can help prevent unnecessary expenses and free up funds for unexpected costs.

4. Insure against potential risks: Evaluate your insurance coverage to ensure you have adequate protection against potential risks. This includes health insurance, auto insurance, homeowners or renters insurance, and possibly additional coverage like disability or life insurance. Having the right insurance can mitigate the financial impact of unexpected events.

5. Prioritize regular maintenance and repairs: Proactively maintain your possessions, such as your home, car, and appliances, to minimize the likelihood of unexpected breakdowns or major repairs. Regular maintenance can help catch issues early and prevent them from escalating into costly emergencies.

6. Research and compare service providers: When faced with unexpected expenses, take the time to research and compare service providers. Obtain multiple quotes or estimates for necessary repairs or services to ensure you are getting the best value for your money.

7. Revisit your financial plan regularly: Regularly review your financial plan to accommodate any changes or new goals. Assess your emergency fund's adequacy and make adjustments if

necessary. Additionally, consider the impact of unexpected expenses on your long-term financial goals and make any needed adaptations.

8. Stay calm and adapt: Unexpected expenses can be stressful, but staying calm and adaptable is key. Take a deep breath, assess the situation, and explore potential solutions. Consider negotiating payment plans, seeking financial assistance, or exploring alternative options to manage unexpected expenses effectively.

By implementing these strategies, you can develop a proactive approach to handling unexpected expenses, ensuring that you are financially prepared for unexpected challenges that may arise.

Chapter 6

Real Estate Investing Understanding Real Estate Investing

Real estate investing involves the purchase, ownership, management, rental, or sale of properties to generate income and/or capital appreciation. It is a form of long-term investment that can provide various benefits, such as cash flow from rental income, potential tax advantages, diversification of the investment portfolio, and the potential for property value appreciation over time. Real estate investors can choose different strategies, including residential properties, commercial properties, or real estate investment trusts (REITs). Successful real estate investing requires careful research, understanding market trends, assessing potential risks and returns, and effective property management. It can be a rewarding investment avenue for those willing to put in the effort, but it also carries inherent risks and requires thorough due diligence.

* **Types of real estate investments**

Real estate investments encompass various options. Residential real estate involves homes and apartments, yielding income through rent or appreciation. Commercial real estate includes offices, retail, and industrial properties, with profits from leasing to businesses. Industrial real estate comprises warehouses and manufacturing sites, providing stable income through long-term leases.

Retail real estate features shopping centers and retail properties, with rental income from businesses. Multifamily real estate involves apartment complexes, generating rental income from multiple units. Real Estate Investment Trusts (REITs) are publicly-traded companies that own and manage diverse real estate portfolios, offering dividends to shareholders.

* Real estate crowdfunding allows investors to pool resources for various projects via online platforms. Real estate partnerships involve collaborating to invest in properties and share responsibilities and profits. Real estate development entails building or renovating properties for sale or lease. Real estate wholesaling involves securing properties at lower prices and selling them to other investors. Flipping involves buying distressed properties, renovating them, and selling for a profit. Real estate syndication involves experienced investors leading groups to invest in larger properties, sharing returns and risks. Choosing the right type depends on your goals and risk tolerance.

* **Financing real estate investments**

1. Mortgage Loans: Borrowers secure loans from banks or mortgage lenders to purchase properties. These loans can be fixed-rate or adjustable-rate, with varying terms and down payment requirements.

2. Hard Money Loans: These are short-term, high-interest loans from private lenders or investors, often used for property flips or investments where quick cash is needed.

3. Home Equity Loans/HELOCs: Homeowners can tap into the equity in their primary residence to fund real estate investments, using either a home equity loan or a home equity line of credit (HELOC).

4. Private Financing: Investors can seek funds from individuals or private lenders, often offering more flexible terms than traditional banks.

5. Real Estate Syndication: Experienced investors pool money from multiple individuals or entities to fund larger real estate projects, with profits and risks shared among participants.

6. Seller Financing: In some cases, property sellers may offer financing to buyers, allowing them to make payments directly to the seller instead of obtaining a traditional mortgage.

7. Self-Directed IRA/401(k): Investors can use retirement funds to invest in real estate through self-directed accounts, providing tax advantages.

8. Crowdfunding: Online platforms allow investors to contribute small amounts to collectively finance real estate projects.

9. Partnerships: Investors can partner with others to combine resources and share financing responsibilities.

10. REITs: Investing in Real Estate Investment Trusts provides exposure to real estate assets without directly owning property.

Choosing the right financing method depends on factors like the property type, investment goals, creditworthiness, and risk tolerance. Investors should diligently assess their options to identify the most appropriate financing strategy for their real estate investments.

Evaluating potential investments

Certainly, evaluating potential investments is like making smart choices with your money. Imagine you have a jar of jellybeans, and you want to make more jellybeans over time. Each jellybean represents an investment option. Here's how you might evaluate them:

1. Risk: Some jellybeans are easy to hold onto, but others might slip through your fingers. Similarly, some investments are low-risk (like a strong grip on the jellybeans) while others are riskier. You need to decide how many jellybeans you are willing to risk.

2. Return: Think about how many jellybeans you'll get in the future. Some jellybeans grow over time, just like investments that earn you more money. Look for investments that give you more jellybeans later on.

3. Diversification: Do not put all your jellybeans in one jar. It is smarter to spread them into different jars. Likewise, do not put all your money into one investment. Diversifying, or spreading your money across different types of investments, can reduce risk.

4. Time: Some jellybeans take longer to grow, but they might give you more in the end. Similarly, some investments need time to grow and reach their full potential.

5. Costs: Just like some jars have a small opening, some investments have fees that can eat into your jellybean stash. Be aware of these costs.

Remember, making good investment choices is like picking the right jellybeans: you want a balance of safety, growth, and diversity to help your jellybean jar grow over time.

Chapter 7

Taxes

* Understanding tax basics

1. Understanding tax basics is essential for building wealth. By mastering tax principles, you can legally minimize your tax liability, freeing up more money for savings and investments. Here are key tax concepts to grasp:

2. Income Types: Income comes in various forms, such as earned (salaries), passive (rental income), and capital gains (profits from investments). Each is taxed differently, so understanding these distinctions allows you to strategize.

3. Tax Brackets: Tax rates vary based on income levels. Familiarize yourself with your country's tax brackets to optimize your financial decisions within these ranges.

4. Tax Deductions: Identify deductions like mortgage interest, student loan interest, and charitable contributions. These reduce your taxable income, lowering the overall tax burden.

5. Tax Credits: Explore available tax credits, which directly reduce your tax bill. Common ones include the Child Tax Credit or Earned Income Tax Credit.

6. Investment Taxes: Understand how investments are taxed. Long-term investments often receive preferential rates, incentivizing a buy-and-hold strategy.

7. Retirement Accounts: Maximize contributions to tax-advantaged retirement accounts like 401(k)s or IRAs. These offer tax benefits while helping you save for the future.

8. Tax Planning: Regularly review your financial situation to adapt to changing tax laws and life circumstances. Consulting a tax professional can provide tailored guidance.

Incorporating tax strategies into your financial planning can accelerate wealth accumulation and secure your financial future.

* **Filing taxes**

Filing taxes strategically can be a key component of building wealth over time. Here are some tips for using the tax filing process to your advantage:

1. Maximize Deductions: Ensure you take advantage of all available deductions, such as mortgage interest, student loan interest, and medical expenses. Itemizing deductions can often result in significant savings.

2. Contribute to Retirement Accounts: Contribute the maximum allowable amount to tax-advantaged retirement accounts like 401(k)s and IRAs. These contributions not only reduce your taxable income but also allow your investments to grow tax-free until withdrawal.

3. Capital Gains and Losses: Be mindful of capital gains taxes. If you have both gains and losses, consider selling investments strategically to offset gains with losses, reducing your overall tax liability.

4. Tax-Efficient Investing: Invest in tax-efficient funds or assets, like index funds or tax-efficient ETFs, which tend to generate fewer taxable events compared to actively managed funds.

5. Consider Tax Credits: Investigate tax credits available to you, such as the Earned Income Tax Credit or child-related credits. These can directly reduce your tax bill.

6. Seek Professional Advice: Consult with a tax professional or financial advisor who can help you create a tax-efficient strategy tailored to your financial goals.

7. Plan Ahead: Do not wait until tax season to think about taxes. Continuously evaluate your financial situation throughout the year to make informed decisions that minimize your tax burden.

* Tax deductions and credits

Tax deductions and credits are both ways to reduce your taxable income and, ultimately, the amount of taxes you owe. However, they work differently:

1. Tax Deductions: Deductions reduce your taxable income, which in turn lowers the amount of income subject to taxation. Some common deductions include mortgage interest, student loan interest, medical expenses, and contributions to retirement accounts like a 401(k) or an IRA. The more deductions you can claim, the less income you'll be taxed on.

2. Tax Credits: Tax credits, on the other hand, directly reduce the amount of taxes you owe. They are often more valuable than deductions because they provide a dollar-for-dollar reduction in your tax liability. Examples of tax credits include the Child Tax Credit, Earned Income Tax Credit, and education-related credits like the Lifetime Learning Credit.

It is important to research and understand the specific deductions and credits that apply to your financial situation, as they can significantly affect your overall tax liability and potentially lead to tax savings. Tax laws can change, so it is a good idea to stay updated on the latest tax regulations or consult with a tax professional for personalized advice.

Tax planning strategies

Tax planning is the process of organizing your financial affairs in a way that minimizes your tax liability while ensuring you comply with tax laws. Here are some tax planning strategies to consider:

1. *Income Splitting*: If you are in a higher tax bracket, consider shifting income to family members in lower tax brackets. This can be done through gifts, investments, or income-sharing arrangements.

2. *Tax-Efficient Investments*: Invest in tax-advantaged accounts like 401(k)s, IRAs, or HSAs. These accounts offer tax benefits such as tax-deferred growth or tax-free withdrawals.

3. *Maximize Deductions*: Take advantage of tax deductions like mortgage interest, student loan interest, and contributions to retirement accounts. Keep good records of eligible expenses.

4. *Tax Credits*: Ensure you claim all eligible tax credits, such as the Child Tax Credit, Earned Income Tax Credit, or education-related credits. These directly reduce your tax liability.

5. *Charitable Giving*: Donate to qualified charities to receive deductions. Consider strategies like donating appreciated assets or setting up a donor-advised fund.

6. *Tax-Loss Harvesting*: Offset capital gains by selling investments that have declined in value to generate capital losses.

7. *Roth Conversions*: Consider converting traditional retirement accounts (like IRAs) into Roth accounts to potentially pay taxes at a lower rate now and enjoy tax-free withdrawals later.

8. *Business Structure*: Choose the right business structure (e.g., sole proprietorship, LLC, S corporation) for your business to optimize tax benefits.

Estate Planning: Plan for the efficient transfer of wealth to heirs through strategies like gifting, trusts, and taking advantage of the estate tax exemption.

9. *Timing*: Be mindful of the timing of income and expenses. Delay income or accelerate deductions when it makes sense from a tax perspective.

10. *Tax-Efficient Withdrawals*: When you are retired, carefully plan how you withdraw funds from various accounts to minimize taxes on your retirement income.

11. *Stay Informed*: Tax laws change, so stay informed about the latest regulations and consult with a tax professional for personalized advice.

Remember that tax planning should align with your financial goals and circumstances. It is often a good idea to work with a tax advisor or financial planner who can help you develop a tax strategy tailored to your specific situation.

Chapter 8

Financial Planning

* The importance of financial planning

Financial planning is crucial for several reasons:

1. Goal Achievement: It helps individuals and businesses define their financial goals and create a roadmap to achieve them. Whether it is buying a home, funding education, or retiring comfortably, financial planning ensures you have a plan in place.

2. Budgeting: It assists in managing income and expenses effectively. By creating a budget, you can allocate resources efficiently, avoid overspending, and save for future needs.

3. Risk Management: Financial planning involves assessing and mitigating financial risks. This includes insurance coverage to protect against unexpected events like accidents or illnesses.

4. Investment Strategy: It helps determine how to invest your money to achieve your financial goals. This includes selecting appropriate investment vehicles based on your risk tolerance and time horizon.

5. Tax Optimization: Effective financial planning includes strategies to minimize tax liabilities. This can result in significant savings over time.

6. Retirement Planning: Planning for retirement is a critical aspect. It ensures that you have enough savings to maintain your desired lifestyle after you stop working.

7. Emergency Funds: Financial planning recommends setting aside funds for emergencies. This provides a safety net in case of unexpected expenses or income disruptions.

8. Debt Management: It helps in managing and reducing debt. Effective debt management strategies can improve your financial health.

9. Estate Planning: For those with significant assets, financial planning includes estate planning to ensure the smooth transfer of wealth to heirs and minimize estate taxes.

10. Peace of Mind: Having a well-thought-out financial plan provides peace of mind. It reduces financial stress and helps you feel more in control of your financial future.

In summary, financial planning is not just about managing money; it is about achieving your life goals, securing your future, and navigating the complex world of personal and business finance with confidence.

* **Creating a financial plan**

Creating a financial plan involves several key steps:

1. Set Clear Goals: Define your short-term and long-term financial goals. These could include buying a house, saving for retirement, paying off debt, or funding your children's education.

2. Assess Your Current Financial Situation: Take a close look at your current income, expenses, assets, and liabilities. This forms the foundation of your financial plan.

3. Create a Budget: Develop a detailed budget that outlines your monthly income and expenses. This will help you track your spending and identify areas where you can save or invest more.

4. Emergency Fund: Ensure you have an emergency fund set up with enough savings to cover at least three to six months of living expenses. This provides a financial safety net.

5. Debt Management: If you have high-interest debts (like credit card debt), create a plan to pay them down systematically. Prioritize paying off high-interest debts first.

6. Investment Strategy: Determine your risk tolerance and investment goals. Create an investment portfolio that aligns with your objectives, whether it is for retirement, education, or wealth accumulation.

7. Tax Planning: Explore tax-efficient strategies to minimize your tax liability. This may involve contributing to retirement accounts, taking advantage of tax credits, or using tax-advantaged investments.

8. Insurance Coverage: Review your insurance policies, including health, life, and property insurance. Ensure you have adequate coverage to protect against unexpected events.

9. Retirement Planning: Calculate how much you need to save for retirement and choose appropriate retirement accounts (e.g., 401(k), IRA) to achieve your retirement goals.

10. Estate Planning: Consider creating or updating your will, naming beneficiaries, and planning for the distribution of your assets after your passing.

11. Regular Review: Your financial plan should be dynamic. Review it periodically, especially when significant life changes occur (marriage, children, job changes). Adjust your plan as needed.

12. Professional Guidance: If you are unsure about certain financial aspects or investments, consult a financial advisor or planner for expert advice.

13. Stay disciplined: Stick to your plan and avoid making impulsive financial decisions. Discipline is key to achieving your financial goals.

14. Monitor Progress: Continuously monitor your financial progress. Use tools and apps to help you track your income, expenses, and investments.

15. Educate Yourself: Stay informed about financial matters. Understanding basic financial concepts empowers you to make informed decisions.

Remember that a financial plan is a personalized roadmap, and it should evolve as your circumstances change. The key is to start planning, even with small steps, and gradually build a stronger financial foundation for your future.

* **Working with a financial advisor**

Collaborating with a financial advisor is a strategic move towards building wealth. These professionals assess your financial landscape, craft personalized plans, and offer expert guidance. They help you define achievable wealth goals, create diversified investment portfolios, optimize taxes, and manage risks. By regularly monitoring and adjusting your strategies, they provide discipline and steer you clear of emotional investment decisions. With their support, you can work towards long-term financial security, making informed choices that align with your objectives, ultimately setting you on a path to accumulate and preserve wealth for the future.

* **Monitoring and adjusting your plan**

Monitoring and adjusting your wealth-building plan is essential for long-term financial success. Regularly track your income, expenses, and investments to ensure you stay on course. Analyze your budget to identify areas where you can cut costs or increase savings. Continuously educate yourself about investment opportunities and adapt your portfolio as needed to align with your financial goals and risk tolerance. Remain flexible and receptive to change, as economic conditions and personal circumstances evolve. Regularly review and adjust your plan to maximize your wealth-building potential and secure a more financially stable future.

Conclusion

Finance can seem daunting, but it is an essential part of our lives. By understanding the basics of finance, you can make informed decisions about your money and build a solid financial future. This book provides an overview of the most important aspects of finance for beginners. Remember to keep learning and make smart choices with your money.

www.ingramcontent.com/pod-product-compliance
Lightning Source LLC
LaVergne TN
LVHW061604070526
838199LV00077B/7173